This book is dedicated to my teacher, Mrs. Johnson.

Copyright © 2022 Jennifer Jones
All copyright laws and rights reserved. Published in the U.S.A.
For more information, email info@ninjalifehacks.tv
Paperback ISBN: 978-1-63731-608-5
eBook ISBN: 978-1-63731-609-2
Hardcover ISBN: 978-1-63731-610-8

Find the Rulers on Strike lesson plans at ninjalifehacks.tv

It's much easier to do when you have a ruler nearby. You can run your pencil against our straight edge spine.

They fling us and throw us across the classroom. They scrape us on the floor as if we are brooms.

The teacher explained to the students how they had treated us in awful ways. We were prepared to leave them for the rest of the school days!

When the students said sorry,
we decided to talk it all out.
We told them how we felt,
what our strike was all about.